# Say Yes 2 Your Life

## Journey to Celebrate Your "is-ness"

Sally Orcutt, OP

Write Way Publishing Company

Say Yes 2 Your Life: Journey to Celebrate Your "is-ness"

Copyright © 2017 by Sally Orcutt

All rights reserved. No part of this publication may be reproduced, distributed, or transmitted in any form or by any means, including photocopying, recording, or other electronic or mechanical methods, without the prior written permission of the publisher, except in the case of brief quotations embodied in critical reviews and certain other noncommercial uses permitted by copyright law. Permission requests should be sent to info@writewaypublishingcompany.com.

Printed in the United States of America

ISBN 978-1-946425-02-7

Cover and interior graphics design by Annie Flood Design

Book design by CSinclaire Write-Design

Write Way Publishing Company LLC

## *Testimonials*

*Say Yes 2 Your Life* is a powerful call to find our "is-ness." From core values to personal strengths to the superhero within, Sally Orcutt opens our eyes to the wonder that lies within each of us. If you are searching for your purpose in life, this book holds the key to finding it. If you already know your "is-ness," this title shows you how to stretch yourself and grow.
— Annie Morecambe, author of *The Legends of Greywinds*

*Say Yes 2 Your Life* is an amazing adventure into finding yourself and discovering the light you carry inside. We are all here for a purpose and, sadly, so many of us get lost on the way to finding it. Sally is masterful in walking you through the steps to finding your special "is-ness" and putting your love out into the world. Her personal story resonates the warmth to let you know you are on the journey with someone who has been there and done that.
— Stephanie McDilda, President, Flashpoint International

Sally has nailed this one! This book is vital to discovering your authentic self, it's life-changing and liberating. A reference book that will perpetually lift and free you to live life to the fullest.
— Deneane Stanley-Sutton, Deputy Director
The Stanley House of L.O.V.E.

# Dedication

I dedicate this book to my mom. You said I was the "wind beneath your wings" and you were that for me as well. You helped me see my gifts when I couldn't. You gave me the courage to shine and trust myself when I struggled to find my voice.

# Table of Contents

Preface. . . . . . . ix

Acknowledgments. . . . . . xv

Introduction. . . . . . . 3

**Chapter 1:** My Story. . . . . . 13

**Chapter 2:** Are You Ready for a Mind Shift?. . 27

**Chapter 3:** Finding Your "is-ness". . . . . . 41

**Chapter 4:** What's Your Super Power? . . . 53

**Chapter 5:** Why Saying Yes Matters. . . . . 69

**Chapter 6:** Unleashing Your Superhero . . . 81

Epilogue. . . . . . 93

Resources. . . . . . 99

About the Author. . . . . 101

# Preface

It's not what you are that is holding you back. It's what you think you are not.

*(Anonymous)*

**W**hy did I write this book? Because the life I had, a life that I desperately clung to for more than 40 years had disappeared. It was a life that had wonderful moments of joy and laughter but also a life that was filled with chronic self-doubt and insecurity. With my mother's death, my life changed. In the moment that old life disappeared, I felt lost, adrift, and completely isolated. I found it difficult to do something as simple as breathe. The only thing I seemed to be any good at was sobbing. I wallowed in the pain of my loss because I was afraid. Afraid to consider what life would be now.

The life in which my mother held my sense of positive self-worth was the only life I had known since I was 10 years old. How would I make sense out of the life that was left to me? I went to work, took care of my children, and did all the regular activities of daily life. But I was empty inside. I didn't know how to fill the gaping hole in my life. I had no words to describe that feeling with anyone else and felt sure they would think I was crazy if I tried.

Finally, after four years of suffering in lonely isolation, slowly, ever so slowly, I began to let the outside world touch me again. My sister saved my life. I believe God sends us the angels we need. Laurie was the angel He sent to help me crawl back into my life again. Family knows us in a way that, sometimes, we don't even know ourselves. She offered me the chance to be part of something that helped me make a positive difference for women. She needed me, she said. The truth is I needed her. I needed to be part of her organization. I was being led on a journey to build a new life. The life I live today. And each time I said yes to an opportunity that called to me, I learned more about me. Who I was and what really mattered to me. Looking back, it was as though I had gone into a protective cocoon during those four years when I couldn't face life.

As I began to say yes, I slowly became a beautiful butterfly. Like the caterpillar, I dissolved into a "Sally soup." The life I had before ended. And like a butterfly from the cocoon, I emerged from my old self into the powerful woman I am today. Neither caterpillars nor people go into the cocoon and suddenly sprout butterfly wings. The old life ceases to exist in its previous form. I was still a mother, sister, co-worker, and friend. But I emerged from my "Sally soup" as a new creation.

When I became this new creation, the chronic self-doubt faded away. My decisions were no longer influenced by what I perceived others expected of me. I began to say yes to who I am and claim my authentic life. I left my old life, that life I had desperately tried to hang on to because I couldn't imagine another way, that life in which I was so quick to believe I was not good enough, that I needed to change. My old life has been replaced with a life I hadn't really considered since I was 10 years old. A life that doesn't involve comparisons. A life that recognizes I have unique gifts to share. It's a life that gets excited about possibilities and ideas even when I find myself stretching my comfort zone beyond what I once believed possible. *I love this life.* I know I have an *"is-ness"* that only I can bring into this world. And the world needs me to bring it every day! I don't have to fear taking chances on things I want to do because I might not do everything perfectly. All I need to do is be me.

It's been a journey. Maybe even a wild ride at times. I can say for certain that it's a journey worth taking. It has changed my life. This journey has opened my eyes to the life I longed for but wasn't sure how to find. After 40 years, the voices in my head that have ruled my life since I was 10 years old are finally quiet. As I look back at the journey, I realize there were specific touchpoints that helped me along the way. That is why I am writing this book. I want to share those touchpoints with you. I want to shout from the highest mountain, *"You don't have to live with self-doubt. You don't have to change yourself in any way to be loved and to have what you want in life."* It's a journey that began with my mom's death and my sister's love. All I had to do to complete the journey was say *YES* to my life. You can do this too. I'm looking forward to sharing this journey with you.

# Acknowledgments

When I decided to write this book, it was part of the answer to a call I heard from God to share His message that we are all beloved and wonderfully gifted just as we are. I am so grateful that He called me to do this work. It brings me joy even as it expands my comfort zone beyond what I ever imagined possible.

My ability to share this journey was made possible by so many people who have loved and supported me during this project.

First on that list is my wonderful husband Paul. He has remained supportive throughout this adventure and never complained when my getting up at 5:30 in the morning interrupted his sleep. Paul is the love of my authentic life. I met him as I began to understand who I was and the gifts I have been given to share. Thank you, *Honna Honna,* for your patience and letting me be me.

My sons Garrett and Bryan who are the two greatest gifts I have been given in my life. You are both amazing young men, and I am incredibly proud of who you are. You have both encouraged me greatly as I reinvented my life.

My sister Laurie, you are an amazing woman. Thank you for being you. Thank you for talking me off the proverbial ledge when I feel overwhelmed. You help me find balance when my life occasionally spins a little out of control.

I want to thank my Lay Dominican Community and the Dominican friars for their loving support as I continued to search for my voice. From the moment I attended the first meeting, I knew I was home. I am convinced that God puts in our path the people we need to meet to walk with us on our journey. You have all taught me so much, and I love the path we are traveling together to share God's message of unconditional love.

Barbara Pegg who reminded me that I need to be authentic and write this book from the perspective of who I am as a Catholic and a Lay Dominican. You made the writing easier as I was able to just be me.

Sterling Fulton and Stephanie McDilda—you both inspire me with the work you are doing. You are my idea "popcorn poppers" and spark ideas in me that I know I wouldn't get to on my own. I value the relationship I have with each of you and look forward to years of collaboration on workshops and presentations.

My wonderful Beta Readers—Stephanie, Karen, Deneane, Sally, and Ryanne. You all added tremendous value and made the book better. Thank you for your insights and your willingness to be part of this project.

And I want to thank all those who shared their stories with me. You are all amazing women who are saying yes to your lives and your gifts. I celebrate all that you do.

# Say Yes
## 2 Your Life

# *Introduction*

The life you want begins the moment you embrace the life you have because all of it is a miracle.

*(Rob Bell)*

**S**ay Yes 2 Your Life is for people at all stages of their journey to accepting, acknowledging, and loving themselves. It is a road map for those just considering or beginning the journey; it provides reinforcement for longtime journeyers; and it is a tool for people already far along on their journeys who are looking for ways to share and pass on what they have learned.

Growing in authenticity is not another self-improvement project. It's about finding your "is-ness" and creating a life that honors who you are at the very depths of your being. The person you were before you were a friend, a spouse, a parent. The person you were before you held this position or volunteered for that organization. Who you are is who you are. And understanding who you are is at the heart of loving and accepting yourself. It is also at the heart of understanding your "why" and what you are being called to do in *this* moment. Because wherever you are in this moment of your life, you are being called to share the gifts that are uniquely you.

Honoring your "is-ness" means owning your strengths *and* your weaknesses. It's about learning that you can achieve anything you want in life and about accepting that you will benefit from receiving the gift of another's "is-ness" along the way. The journey is about guiding you on a path to silence the voice in your head that says, "Play it safe. Don't risk making a mistake. Someone else can do it better than you." As you travel this road, you will realize that saying yes to living authentically means saying no to making comparisons. You will begin to integrate your whole self and love who you are, just as you are. You will claim the truth that you have everything you need within you to have the life you desire. This book will be your companion as you discover or rediscover your core self and begin exploring new ways to share all you have to offer.

Throughout this book I'll share stories from those who have already begun the journey. The journey I know best is my own, so many of the stories I'll share are from my own life. However, as this book was coming to life, I had the opportunity to speak with a number of women who are in different stages of their own journey, and I have included parts of their stories as well. For years, I believed I was the only person who suffered from often debilitating self-doubt. A belief that made me feel inadequate and often very alone. It is very difficult to share with someone else that you feel worthless. Who wants to admit that to another person? However, this book is not about me. It is not about the other women I spoke with. Each of these stories is included for one simple reason. I want you to trust in this truth:

If you suffer from self-doubt, you are not alone.

**No comparison zone**

As I listened to the women I met, I became very aware that my story, although painful for me, at times felt insignificant by comparison to their stories. For a brief moment, I questioned whether I had a right to share my journey and whether those who had lived through truly horrific events would be able to connect with what I was sharing. I realized, however, that the pain and emotions for myself, as well as the pain and emotions of each of the women I spoke with, were very real. The reason someone finds themselves in the place of feeling that they are not good enough—or they don't deserve to be treated well and have the life they want—doesn't matter. What matters is that it's not true.

One of the gifts you will receive as you say yes to living your authentic life is the deep understanding that comparisons are not useful. When you own your "is-ness," you no longer feel the need to compare yourself to others. So as you read this book, if you find yourself feeling, "My story is so much worse than theirs," I ask you to please accept that these stories are not in competition or in comparison with each other. Your story is your story. The impact it had on your life is real. When you compare your story with others, it can be easy to believe that nobody can understand how you feel because your story is so horrible. However, based on the women I've spoken with, I'm convinced that if we are honest with ourselves, we'll agree there is at least one person out there whose story is "worse" than ours. Regardless of what caused each of us pain, the pain did and perhaps still does impact the way we choose to live our lives. We will grow stronger in our commitment to ourselves and to each other as we own the truth that it doesn't matter what made us feel we are not enough. Anything that makes us feel devalued leaves us with the same emotion - unworthiness.

**Willingness to consider change**

The first touchpoint of your journey is the willingness to consider change in your life. Change is really difficult for most of us even when what we are changing from isn't working for us. We want something new, but instead of doing what it takes to get what we want, we use an enormous amount of energy convincing ourselves why what we've got isn't so bad. I heard a speaker share this piece of wisdom several years back, "If you're riding a dead horse, the best strategy is to dismount. However, we hate change so we keep trying to explain to ourselves, as well as to others, why the 'dead horse' is really not so bad after all." Oh, how true that has been in my life. What about you? Can we agree it is time to dismount?

Dismounting will require us to change our automatic habits and thought responses. If you're like me, you know changing any habit is not as simple as flipping a switch. Our brains prefer to run on autopilot. Not only are they hardwired to protect us from danger, they are also hardwired to do the least amount of work possible. I learned that the human brain has a limited amount of energy to expend each day, and it takes a set amount of energy just to "keep the lights on" (aka keep our bodies running). In fact, research done by scientists at Duke University found that more than 40 percent of the actions we take every day have nothing to do with conscious decisions. They are habits. This allows the brain to conserve energy just in case at the end of the day we suddenly find ourselves in a "fight or flight" position and the brain needs to make an important decision. What this means for our decision-making process is that instead of our brain trying to figure out how to react to every situation in our day, it uses predefined pathways based on *similar* situations. Our brain recognizes a similar situation and just operates on cruise control. This includes both physical and verbal triggers.

Many of these predefined pathways or neural grooves go back to input we received between the ages of 7 and 11 years old. At that stage of our development, we are very literal, and the messages we hear and the images we see shape our belief systems deeply. This includes our belief system about ourselves. After spending years responding to a specific situation or a specific verbal trigger in the same way, our brain will automatically respond to similar situations in the same way. Think about the Grand Canyon. For thousands of years, the Colorado River has been cutting through the path that has made the Grand Canyon what it is today. And, while our automatic responses have not been forming brain pathways for that length of time, the longer we continue to respond automatically to specific situations, the deeper the grooves in our brain become. When we *choose* a different response, we actually create a new groove or pathway in our brain. We are retraining our brain to react in a different way to a familiar stimuli. It's not always easy, but it absolutely can be done. The old pathway is still there, but the more we exercise the new pathway, the stronger it becomes until that pathway becomes the automatic response.

I now understand why my first *really* big YES, the yes that resulted in my leaving my job and becoming an entrepreneur, was so difficult for me. I had spent more than 40 years of my life reacting to situations that involved risk by running the other way. Running was my automatic response, and I was deeply attached to that reaction. Until it became too excruciating to continue on that dead horse, I refused to dismount.

Eventually though, I got off. The changes I've made in my life are ones you can make too. All you need to do is say yes and you'll be on your way. If you're like me, you'll never look back.

## How to read this book

There is no right way to read this book. You may decide to read it all the way through and then come back and reflect on each section. You may decide to jump directly to a chapter that speaks to you most compellingly in this moment. The choice is yours. Each chapter takes you through a specific part of the journey.

We'll begin by talking about the voices that influence our lives. For many of us, the negative "inner critic" has been the controlling voice in our lives. But there is, *and always has been*, another voice—the voice that knows you can do anything you really want in life. We'll take some time to get reacquainted with that voice.

Next, we'll do an exercise to guide you through a discovery, or maybe rediscovery, of your core values and unique gifts. What I like to call your "is-ness" or superpower. We each have a superhero inside us that is longing to make a difference and express our unique way of bringing more love into the world. You will be amazed when you see how your superhero has been showing up in your life even when you didn't recognize it.

I wish I could see the smile on your face as you have your aha moment and realize how many lives you have touched. The moment we realize how positively we impact others is very powerful. When you can put a face and a name to someone whose life you touched through the sharing of your gifts, you understand how very important it is for you to share your gifts with those around you.

Finally, you will begin to explore some of those dreams you may have put on hold because you felt "you couldn't do it" and visualize the steps you can take to make your dream(s) a reality.

The journey to living an authentic life takes some time. I am confident that once you commit to getting on the path, you will begin to feel the spark of what is possible for you very quickly. Please don't take shortcuts. I will be asking you to write and journal along the way. This is important. Researchers have found several benefits to writing down things. One of the most important benefits associated with your journey is the opportunity to learn, process, and reframe information in a new way. In fact, researcher Stanislas Dehaene, a psychologist at the College de France in Paris said, "When we write, a unique neural circuit is automatically activated. There is core recognition of the gesture in the written word, a sort of recognition by mental stimulation of the brain." This research validates the truth I experienced on my journey toward discovering my authentic self and accepting my gifts. Therefore, these chapters contain exercises and places to journal, draw, and express yourself. There are also reflection questions at the end of many of the chapters. Please give yourself the time to reflect, journal, discover, and dream as you travel on your journey. It is an important part of finding and honoring all that is really you.

## What to expect

I want to caution you not to be discouraged if you find yourself taking two steps forward toward a goal and one step back. This is natural. Remember those brain pathways. They want to go back to the familiar. Celebrate every small step you achieve, every little success along the way. That may mean you applaud the fact you were authentically you for a day, an hour, and sometimes just 5 minutes.

Try not to focus on how much of the journey you feel you still need to travel. As you continue along the path, each yes helps you build momentum for the next one. You will find over time that the backward steps don't happen as often or take you as far back down an unproductive path. Each time you say yes to your authentic life, it allows you to become more fully alive. Each yes gives you greater insight into the treasure of your true self. And, once you identify your unique gifts and recognize how important it is to those around you that you share those gifts, you will gain the energy to explore the dreams you hold within you.

## Language and belief systems

*I* wrestled with what would be the correct language to use in this book. I wanted to be inclusive so initially I thought I would use only non-spiritual language. I believe the journey to say yes to your life crosses all boundaries of race, culture, and religion, and I didn't want to make it difficult for anyone to hear what I was trying to share because I used words they found challenging or difficult to hear. However, several people reminded me that this is a book about living an authentic life. If I chose to remove any references to my personal belief system, what would that say about my belief in living authentically?

I believe we are all guided on our life journey. Depending on what your belief system is, you might call that guide God, Spirit, inner voice, higher power, or any one of a number of other names that has meaning for you. For me, that guide is God and Spirit. Throughout the book there will be times that I will use that language. It is my intent to do so only where I feel it is important to the story I am sharing. In those instances, I ask and encourage you to hear those words through your own belief system.

Those who know me know that I always seek to be inclusive. I look for the ways in which we are the same rather than seeking to find differences. Because living authentically means accepting ourselves for exactly who we are, part of being authentic means we are free to speak our truth using the language that is authentic for each of us. And because we understand that we are not in a comparison or competition, we are able to hear the language of others as the way they express their authentic truth.

# Reflections

*What is one change you would like to make in your life today? What is the "dead horse" you've been convincing yourself is not "so bad after all?"*

_____

_____

_____

_____

*What is one of your "Grand Canyon" neural pathways? What is one automatic response you would like to change?*

_____

_____

_____

_____

## Chapter 1: My Story

Explore your mind, discover yourself, then give the best that is in you to your age and to your world. There are heroic possibilities waiting to be discovered in every person.

*(Wilfred Peterson)*

My new life began the day my mother died, October 18th, 2002.

Does that sound crazy? It's true. My mom was my very best friend and the only person I ever felt loved me unconditionally. She believed in me. She held my sense of value and self-worth for most of my life. I had lived with a deep-seated self-doubt since I was 10 years old. At that time, I was judged not by what I had accomplished but how I compared to my older brother. In that moment, I started comparing myself to others and believed my value was measured not by what I did, but by what others thought about me.

My mom's belief in me was the anchor I could always count on to find validation. She saw in me what I had stopped seeing in myself. So the day my mom died, I not only lost my mother and best friend, I lost the only voice I could count on to tell me I was wonderful and good. I was desperate. How was I going find my way now? The only voice I had left was the one in my head. The one that reminded me I needed to prove my worth every day.

I was really afraid; so afraid that I retreated into myself for nearly four years. To the outside world, my life looked fine. But most of the time I was just going through the motions. It took years, but slowly my new life began and I heard a new voice that came from deep within me gradually surfacing to a place where I could listen. It's a voice that was always there but one I had ignored.

This voice I rediscovered encourages me to say yes to who I am. It reminds me when I start the old comparison games that God loves me. I am not perfect and I don't have to be. All I have to do is be me. After letting my mom hold my sense of self-value for 40 years, I now hold my own sense of value and self-worth. And when I think about where I've been and the life I have now, I want to shout YES!!! And share the journey.

**The road to comparisons**

So, what happened when I was 10? I got a B in English. That doesn't sound so traumatic. But it was.

When I got my report card, I was so excited. I had earned four As as well as a B in English. I always had a mix of As and Bs but this report card was *really* good. I couldn't wait to show my parents. It was the end of the day, so I didn't have to wait very long to share this good news with my mom. She always picked up me, my sister, and my brothers from school. She gave me a hug and told me how proud she was of me. I was beaming.

My dad worked in the city, so I had to wait for him to get home to show him my report card. I was nervously excited all through dinner. My dad did not give praise easily. You had to really do something to get words of approval from him. I was sure this report card would win me a smile and congratulations.

After dinner, I grabbed my report card and sat down next to him on the couch. "I got my report card, Dad," I said. He took the report card and began looking at it. I was smiling and shifting side to side like kids do, anticipating what he would say. And then he spoke. "Your brother wouldn't have gotten a B in English."

That was nearly 50 years ago, but I still remember how I felt. The breath went out of me. I vaguely remember him adding, as an afterthought, that yes, this was a good report card. But as far as I was concerned, those words didn't matter. I heard loud and clear that I was not as good as my brother. I was not being measured by how well I had done. I was being compared to someone else. I had not measured up.

Until that moment I had not considered that I was being compared. Sure, we kids would have rivalries. That's what kids do. But I had always believed that if I did my best that was all I needed to do. In that moment everything changed. I started down a path that continued for over 40 years. I measured myself against everyone, which led to judging myself and others. I avoided taking chances because I was afraid that if I didn't get everything exactly right, I would open myself up to critique.

Words have such power. They carry enormous weight and can impact our lives for decades. I'm reminded of a line in the Barbara Streisand movie, *The Mirror has Two Faces*. The character she played lives most of her life believing she is not beautiful. Sitting at the kitchen table with her mother she says, "I don't think I would have thought I was not beautiful except you told me my nose was too big."

The power of words. I'm certain my dad didn't mean for his words to impact me the way they did, but they did. For the next 40 years, I pushed myself constantly to avoid the feeling of being told I had fallen short. I lived life trying to prove I was better than others. It wasn't about doing what I imagined for myself at all. I didn't really give that much thought. One of the stories I share that is funny now, but was deadly serious at the time, is the process I went through during my senior year in high school as I tried to decide on my college major. It went like this:

"I got a D- in French and a D in Chemistry, I think I'll major in Chemistry."

Right about this point, anyone listening when I tell this story starts laughing and maybe thinking about crazy choices they've made too. You see, my older brother, the one who would never have gotten a B in English, was studying Engineering. And while I didn't dare compete head-on with him, I thought my dad would be impressed that I was studying something really difficult as well. I imagined that if I made the Dean's List for Chemistry and graduated with honors, my dad would think I was the one on top.

I spent four years of my life driving myself incredibly hard to win a competition that nobody except me was even aware existed. I studied constantly, pushing myself nonstop. I read and re-read each chapter of my textbooks until I knew the information cold. When it finally came time to graduate, the magnitude of what I had done suddenly dawned on me. My dad didn't say anything. I guess he expected me to do well. My brother wasn't even aware that I was competing with him for glory and praise.

Now I had a degree in something that I absolutely didn't want to make into a career. I can laugh about it today. But at the time, it was incredibly humbling. I had just spent four years trying to be Geoff-like. I'd like to tell you that moment of realization changed things for me. But I kept riding that dead horse thinking, "I just need to find a different way to win approval." In fact, I got pretty good at convincing myself that a life of trying to prove yourself wasn't that bad.

**No going back**

After my mom died, I was forced to find a new life. My sister helped me crawl out from beneath the rock of my own self-pity and, as I re-awakened to the world, something caught my attention. My church was offering a year-long program in social justice called Just Faith. I have always felt drawn to helping those less fortunate so the idea appealed to me. I had plenty of time on my hands. My children were teenagers and pretty self-sufficient. I thought, "Why not give this a try?" I felt a strong need to be part of something bigger than myself.

The class met once a week and involved reading, volunteering, and group discussions on social justice. Starting the program was a first step to saying yes to the life I would come to live. But it was my willingness to listen to the urging of the Spirit who told me to stay even when the dynamics of the group became increasingly difficult for me. Staying was life-changing. More than half the class dropped out because of some underlying conflicts within the group. I almost did. *Three times.* But deep within me, I knew it was important that I finish the program. And I'm glad I did. Living through that time of struggle taught me an important lesson. Even when you know you are on the right path, things don't go smoothly all the time.

When the course was finished, we were invited to participate in a Social Justice Ministry Fair. It was a good opportunity to meet people from different organizations. After all, the plan was to now find our place in the volunteering world. I was on fire with a desire to help others and make a difference. That made it all the more frustrating for me when nothing seemed like the right fit. With each new idea I came across, I would go to several meetings, raise my hand saying yes I can do that, and then become disenchanted with the work and realize it was not for me. I don't remember the names of each of the organizations I tried to connect with during that time. What I do remember is that as important as each opportunity was and the good that it did, it wasn't what I felt called to do, and I couldn't find the energy or enthusiasm to move forward. I felt like such a failure. The old and familiar negative voice in my head started telling me that I was a quitter. That I still couldn't get it right. But that small voice inside called to me again and again. It said, *"You are not a failure.* These ministries are just not what you are being called to do."

What I realized, although I was a bit shy to admit it to all those who were serving the poor both in the United States and across the world, is that the individuals I felt I was being called to help and encourage were ones who didn't necessarily belong to any particular group.

Yes, the primary intent of the Just Faith program seemed to be bringing into focus ways we can uplift people on the fringes of society. I understand this and recognize the importance of lifting up those who are marginalized in our society. But who decides who those people are? I still get chills when I remember the moment I realized what I was being called to do. I am here to encourage people like me who suffer from a poverty of self-image. Individuals who desperately need to have someone be a voice that says "you are special just as you are."

Unlike the people we've all met who appear to suffer from delusions of grandeur, there are those of us who suffer from the delusion that we do not matter. This was my calling. It wasn't exciting. Maybe it wasn't even noticeable to others. But it was right for me. It satisfied the longing in my heart to first of all notice others and then, where possible, be a voice of encouragement.

Being truly aware is, I believe, the greatest gift I can offer another human being. It validates that they are worthwhile, special, and valuable. They are beloved. And they are beloved just because they exist, just the way they are. Belovedness is not something any of us can earn. It just is. All I have to do to live my calling is be aware. I have the chance to meet the people on street corners, in the store, in church, at my job, or the park who need to hear the message that they are important. Like me for so many years, most of them look just fine on the outside. But when you listen, really listen, they often have empty, sorrowful places on the inside. I learned another important lesson: Saying yes is not always about doing big things. It's about doing your thing.

During this time, a friend introduced me to the Lay Dominicans of Raleigh, a community within the Roman Catholic Church and the Order of Preachers. As I attended meetings and learned more about the group, I realized that being a Lay Dominican might let me explore the call I felt to speak to individuals who weren't the focus of a particular social justice mission. I was being invited to commit myself to a life of prayer, study, community, and preaching.

While it was the idea of preaching or sharing the message of belovedness that appealed to me, my old nemesis (aka my negative voice) was alive and well and parked on my shoulder. The preaching part scared me to death! Thankfully, the path to becoming a permanently professed Lay Dominican takes years. I didn't have to make an immediate decision.

For six years I kept going, even though I wasn't completely sure what it would mean for me to preach. As I drew closer to the day I was to make my permanent profession, I panicked. I believed preaching as a Lay Dominican would give me the platform to be a voice of encouragement to individuals wherever I met them. But could I do it? As much as I believed in my heart that this was what I was called to do, I wasn't completely sure that I would have the ability to get past my feeling of not being good enough.

I bolted. I left the community to "think" for about four months. Then in the Spring of 2014, I realized that, like the Just Faith call, I was being called to a new life. Turning back really wasn't an option. I decided to say yes, to make my permanent promise to Lay Dominican life. I remember that day clearly. Those there with me said they were deeply moved by the strength of my voice. This taught me that when a goal is not just an idea of the moment but a call forward into greater "is-ness," the strength and courage to reject the voice of self-doubt will come.

I've told you that saying yes is a journey. Even though I was already on my journey, it accelerated after I made my permanent profession. In choosing to become a Lay Dominican, it seems as though I gave God permission to use me for his work. That yes in August of 2014 led to perhaps the biggest yes of all two months later. It was the yes that has changed every day of my life since.

On the night of October 22, 2014, I went to bed not feeling any different than other nights before or since. That night I had a dream. In it I was arguing with God. The dream was incredibly powerful and very clear. I felt God was calling me to leave my current job to help others. I have served in different ministries for 15 years. I was now a Lay Dominican offering workshops and retreats. But the calling I felt in this dream, this was asking a lot. While I was sleeping, it seemed like God was telling me to take on the challenge of leaving my current job to serve Him in a new way. He assured me that all would be well. I made several counteroffers trying to convince Him that I could still do what He was asking while staying in my current job. He was persistent. He promised me that the work He had for me to do would bring me happiness. I countered with, "I can't leave a well-paying job. That's nuts!" We went back and forth for what seemed like the whole night. When my alarm went off in the morning, I was exhausted. I turned to my husband Paul and said, "I really think I need to cut back on my hours at work." Notice I said "cut back," not quit. He agreed, confident we would figure out the financial part. I think he could see this was not just some passing idea I had. This was serious.

I arranged with my boss to cut back to a four-day week and began anticipating the new work I would do. You know that feeling when you are doing something that just gives you joy? That is how I felt on my first "Ministry Day," which is what I decided to call my free day off from work. I was ready to begin this new chapter of my life. Until lunch. My husband came home early that day. I could tell there was something wrong. "What happened?" I asked. He answered, "I just got laid off from my job."

I went into a tailspin. As I was trying to process what he was telling me, all I could think about was that I had just cut back my hours and salary and now Paul was out of work. I sat and listened to him share what had happened and then as he went to file unemployment, I told him I was going to go in to work and see if I could get back to 40 hours a week. We were going to have to pay for benefits and would need the extra money. I guess my yes to the new ministry had been only a maybe. I wasn't ready yet. But I soon would be.

I got my hours back and quickly returned to working full-time as if nothing had happened. But it had. I had changed. I had said yes to something I felt called to do. And the fact that I had backed away from it at the first sign of difficulty didn't change that.

From November until May, I became more and more miserable at my job. I became desperate inside and began falling into a deep depression. Paul was still out of work so I felt compelled to stay at my job. I was convinced we needed the security of my steady paycheck to survive, while at the same time I felt crushed under the weight of that belief. Why?

Because I had seen something else. I had seen what my life could be like. Then, I turned my back on it and shut the door. Tightly. Things between Paul and me got more and more tense. My misery became so intense I would occasionally pound Paul's chest like a wounded animal screaming, "I don't know what to do! I can't do this anymore!"

He wanted me to leave the job and follow my dream. I was scared to take that risk. I couldn't. We needed the money. We needed the security of my job.

For months, I endured the battle waging in my soul. I couldn't let myself take the leap of faith needed to leave my job. And then, finally, on the morning of May 20, 2015 as I drove to work, I pointed my finger toward heaven and said, "Okay, I'll do it your way. I'm leaving this job." It was like the weight of the world had been lifted. After all those months of misery, I suddenly felt a profound peace fill my entire being. I hadn't figured out what I would do next, but I wasn't worried about that anymore. I had said yes. God was going to have to help me figure out the rest.

I left my job on June 30th to open my own business, and I have never regretted that decision or looked back. The peace I felt in making the decision carried me through as I made my plans and did the work of getting prepared for a new work life. I was filled with a sense of knowing what was truly important to me.

Friends supported my choice but still had questions. My friend Barb, who knew how much I had struggled in my job, asked me one day if I was running toward or away from something. I told her with surety, "I have finally stopped running away from what I know I need to do."

It was incredible how sure I felt of my new direction. Some people told me that I was incredibly brave. I wasn't sure how to tell them that I didn't feel brave. I was doing what I needed to do. My dream, nearly eight months before, had opened my mind and my heart to what my life could be like if I would stop trying to live according to what I thought other people expected of me. Instead, I could focus on what truly mattered to me. Through all of this, I learned that when you follow your dream, whatever it is, you will know you are on the right path. You will feel that sense of peace that is bigger than the questions you might still have.

## Reflections

*Have you ever felt as though you were just going through the motions in your life? Describe what was going on and why you felt this way.*

_____

_____

_____

_____

_____

*What words have had a strong impact on your life? What actions have you taken as a result of those words?*

_____

_____

_____

_____

_____

*What's your dream? Is there something you've felt drawn to that maybe you haven't tried yet?*

_____

_____

_____

_____

_____

# Chapter 2:
# Are You Ready For a Mind Shift?

> Why compare yourself to others? No one in the entire world can do a better job of being you than you.
>
> *(Unknown)*

At the foundation of living a more authentic life is the willingness to change thought patterns you've probably been using most of your life. We all can picture that familiar image of the angel and the devil sitting on opposite shoulders trying to influence our choices. Undergoing this mind shift does not mean that you will eliminate that doubting voice in your head. I wish it did. But from what I've experienced, both of these voices are always present. However, the negative voice, the voice that has likely been louder or stronger, the voice that has probably convinced you to play it safe and do what others expect and want you to do, will no longer rule your life.

As you face your fears and embrace your "is-ness," you will find yourself, as I did, telling that inner critic to *back off*. And it will. That was huge for me. Keeping that negative voice in check continues to give me such freedom in my life. This mind shift will let the yeses come more and more easily.

As I have grown in knowing who I am, I have become more confident in the life I am living. I see the possibilities of doing the things that make me feel alive. You will too. So, let's look at the thoughts we want to leave behind and the ones we want to claim. Once you start to make that mind shift, you are on your way.

*Sally Orcutt*

## Letting go of comparisons

**W**e're all well aware of the voice in our head that questions our dreams, goals, and plans. "You can't do that," it says. "What are you thinking?" it shouts. That negative voice is certainly the one that I listened to most of my life. It was fueled by my dad and others who *I believed* found me lacking in some way. As human beings, we are wired to compare ourselves to others. That's just the way it is. But when the comparisons rule our lives, we miss seeing the positive impact we have on the people around us. With each comparison in which we see ourselves as the one who was not good enough, we keep our focus on judging ourselves as inadequate. Then we often try and to make ourselves feel better by acquiring material possessions or sinking into unhealthy addictions. I don't have to tell you they don't work.

Karen is a successful writer and artist today, but she shared with me that it took her a long time to break away from the belief formed in her childhood that she had to achieve something important in order to be considered "enough." She grew up in a home situation that gave her every opportunity to explore her gifts. She was encouraged to find ways to use them. But it was a life focused on achievement, and that was the problem. To an outsider, Karen's life seemed ideal and included a very supportive family. Yet, there was more. In addition to the support, there was a steady dose of critique questioning how well she was living up to her potential. This led to years of chronic self-assessment and judgment.

When you say yes to who you are, adequate and gifted, you learn to let go of continuous comparisons. You recognize that comparisons are counterproductive, even harmful. As you deepen your understanding of your own gifts, you realize there is no longer a need to measure yourself against other people. As you begin to embrace your gifts and your unique superpower, your authentic voice becomes stronger. You stop trying to claim someone else's voice, someone you have convinced yourself is more knowledgeable or profound than you are. You stop saying, "Mary does XYZ better than I. I should let her do it." Instead, you say, "Yes, Mary does XYZ *differently* than I, but people need to hear my voice too." Being comfortable with yourself and the gifts you have to share will allow your voice, your passion, and your message to come through loud and clear. Instead of feeling threatened or inadequate, you feel energized by the ideas that others spark in you and that you spark in them. Collaboration and expansion becomes possible. Are you ready to let go of harmful comparisons in your life?

What is one comparison that you would like to let go of on your journey?

_____

_____

_____

_____

_____

## Letting go of the need to "get it right" every time

**Y**ou will not get everything exactly right every time. Living an authentic life means being willing to let go of the pursuit of perfection. Give yourself permission to make mistakes without beating yourself up. I lived with this need for perfection, or what I considered to be perfection, from the moment I felt I was found lacking because of a B in English. I stopped taking risks. If I didn't think I could do something perfectly, I usually chose not to do it at all. But the truth is, great success is rarely ever achieved without failure. It might be one epic failure. Or a series of failures—such as Edison's 10,000 attempts to create a light bulb or Dyson's 5,126 attempts to invent a bagless vacuum cleaner. Whether we like it or not, failure is a necessary stepping-stone to achieving our dreams.

When I was in my early 40s, I was asked to manage a project after one of my co-workers left the firm. I had been working with this co-worker on the project so even though I didn't have experience managing projects, my boss felt I could handle managing this one. It was one of those times I would have definitely said "No thank you" if I'd had the choice. I appreciated that my boss had confidence in me. And on some level, I did believe I had the managerial skills to take this on, and part of me wanted to. So I quieted the negative voice and said yes. I was determined I was going to do a *perfect job!*

Things went along fine until a deadline approached. It was time for the assistance of others assigned to the project to contribute their part. Close to the deadline, I reminded them of their commitment only to have them acknowledge they had put off the work because they were not entirely sure what to do. They explained they had always worked with the colleague who had left the company and had followed his directions.

This news put me into panic mode. What was I going to do? I did not have the skills to complete that work and my co-worker who was supposed to have those skills admitted he didn't either. I didn't want to tell my boss. I felt that would be admitting I couldn't do the job—that I wasn't "good enough" to complete the project for the client. I put myself in such a state that I completely lost the ability to use my own organizational and planning skills. All I could think about was the fact that this very first time I had been given a project management opportunity, I was going to fail.

Well, eventually I did tell my boss. I had to. I needed his help. He pulled in the resources needed, spoke to the client, and the project got completed. And when we reviewed what had happened on the project, the only constructive criticism he had of what I had done was that I had waited too long to bring him in to help. He was right. I had. And although I certainly didn't tell him this, I knew the reason I delayed was because I had been reluctant to ask him for help. I had felt the need to show that I could do this on my own and get everything exactly right. That need caused me, and ultimately other people, unnecessary stress and worry.

Have you ever resisted asking for help because you didn't want to appear as though you couldn't do something?

_____

_____

_____

_____

_____

Today the need to appear perfect has become a thing of the past for me. I have learned that it is okay to make mistakes and that my best *is* good enough. I've learned that when I'm not sure how to proceed, admitting I need someone else's help to accomplish my goals is not something to fear. I never thought I would be able to say that. Trust me when I tell you that when you begin living your authentic life, you will be able to say that too. As you embrace the life you want, you will take some risks. And with risk, there is the opportunity to make mistakes.

## Owning your positive perception

How often do you get frustrated when something happens that interferes with your plans or prevents you from doing something you were looking forward to? When this happens to me it is usually something completely outside of my control that gets in the way. In the past, I would have become more and more agitated because I was going to be late, somebody I wanted to see canceled their visit, an event I was looking forward to had been postponed, or one of my kids got sick and I had to stay home. The list can go on and on. I'm sure you're already thinking of dozens of times something similar has happened to you. Rationally, we know there is nothing we can do about these situations. But still we get frustrated and replay the situation in our minds. "What could I have done to get a different outcome?"

What are some of the kinds of things that get you all wound up? Do you agree that typically these situations are out of your control?

_____

_____

_____

_____

_____

What if instead of allowing ourselves to be overtaken by frustration, we change things up and turn to positive thinking. Recently I heard a speaker share a trick she uses to help her move into a more positive frame of mind when something happens. She said she has trained herself to think of three good things that centered around the frustration. She gave this example that made me smile. She said, "I was driving to a business meeting, and I got a flat tire. Instead of letting frustration rule, I considered these three things: 1) It wasn't raining. 2) I wasn't on my way to the airport to catch a flight. 3) I wasn't wearing the white suit I had planned on wearing." These kinds of thoughts just put your brain in a whole different mode!

As we bring about our authentic lives, we can use positive thinking strategies like this one. Because our brains have those neural grooves that can so quickly take us down a negative, self-defeating path, we need a strategy like this to yank us off that path as quickly as possible.

Like the woman with the flat tire, we have a choice. Do we let the negative voice in our head have its way saying things like, "See, I told you it wasn't a good idea." Or, do we own a positive perception and tell that voice to *back off* and instead look for the valuable lesson we can take with us on the journey.

When outcomes do not look exactly as we pictured them, it is important to remember that it doesn't mean we have failed. Train yourself to be aware of the lesson you are being offered. Sometimes the lesson is that I have headed down a path too quickly and overlooked important information. But most of the time what I have learned expanded my thinking. I find myself saying, "Yes, that makes this idea even better." It's all in how we choose to frame the events in our lives. Adopting a positive perception lets me pull myself off that doubting path. I remind myself of the last three times I felt frustrated yet still pushed through it. And succeeded! I think about how amazing I felt after I stretched myself. After reflecting on these moments, I realized that in the end, my Sally-ness is all I really need.

To help me bring these positive moments front and center in my mind, I try to find time to journal and capture the "I did it" feeling when I have conquered a new "comfort-zone" expansion moment. I make note of the thoughts I had about why I felt I shouldn't or couldn't, the "say yes" self-talk that propelled me to do it anyway, and the way I felt after I made a new accomplishment. When I look in my journal, there is not a single time that I pushed through those negative voices and have not felt stronger and more confident on the other side.

Owning a positive perception helps create the neural pathways our brains need to change the way we react to triggers that have ruled our lives. Even if you've never journaled before, give it a try. Find a notebook and gather these moments of self-doubt to accomplishment. I'm confident that you will realize the excitement that comes from "yes"!

## A quick note about detours and backsliding

The most significant detour I've taken on this journey was getting deeply involved with helping Sterling create her vision. Sterling is a life coach and the author of *The Brain Trust Planner*. From the moment I heard her speak about her book, I was captivated. The premise of the book is that we need to uncover our core values so we can set goals in alignment with those values. Her research indicated that when goals are in alignment with core values, we are much more likely to achieve them. I had already begun to realize that my calling was to speak to people about living an authentic life—a life centered around their "is-ness" in which they truly understood their core values and unique gifts. Sterling's work fit so well with what I wanted to do. I wanted to help her succeed.

Sterling was forming a corporation and asked me to be a part of that work. As I got deeper and deeper into helping her, I realized this was not my calling. It was Sterling's. If I continued down that path, I would be denying what I knew was mine to do. It takes courage to step away from something that feels so aligned with your calling. The work feels *so close* to your vision, and there is comfort in not going it alone. It makes it easy to convince yourself to become part of someone else's vision. It was extremely difficult for me to back away.

I went back and forth three times stepping away from being part of the company only to come back. Each time I struggled to find the right words to help Sterling understand that as much as I believed in the work she was doing, I couldn't be part of her new company. If I did, it would consume my time. She was disappointed, and I think she was fearful that my backing away would impact her ability to achieve her goals. She really believed I would love the work and gave me so many strong arguments for staying. I was torn. I didn't want to disappoint Sterling. I didn't want to impact our friendship. However, each time I went back, I became more and more upset with myself. Why couldn't I just do what I knew I needed to do? I didn't want to risk the friendship, I didn't want to disappoint, and I felt needed which I really liked. But I knew Sterling's work was not mine to do. And when I finally stepped away, she understood.

As you start leading your authentic life, be prepared for detours like this. As you start saying yes, you open yourself up to new possibilities and a new way of thinking. You will meet people who are involved in work that feels exciting to you. As with my detour with Sterling, the work may be close to what you are beginning to imagine for yourself. It takes time to learn to sift through what is *really* yours to do. If the opportunity feels right, explore it further. Don't be afraid of making a wrong choice or decision. I certainly have traveled a winding path with detours or forks in the road on my journey—forks that I took only to find myself needing to retrace my steps. Each time, however, I learned valuable lessons about myself and what I really felt called to do. And the detours, well, they resulted in my meeting people like Sterling who have been a tremendously positive influence in my life. If you find yourself retracing some of your steps along the journey, try not to get frustrated. It's a natural part of finding your authentic voice.

I want to talk a bit about backsliding. Backsliding is different than taking a detour. Remember my story about "Ministry Fridays"? This was right at the beginning of my journey to saying yes. After my dream, I committed to cutting back to four days a week at my job so I could do more volunteering or ministry work. But the moment the "lack of certainly" emotion was triggered when my husband lost his job, I rushed back to the life I had before. I didn't even give my new yes a second thought. As much as I felt called to move down this path, I had not yet created a new neural groove. In fact, when I look back, I realize I was still operating from my old neural grooves keeping one foot firmly planted in the security of what was familiar. It's no surprise to me now that when my fear of lack of security was triggered, I quickly snapped the other foot back over the line.

Here's a tip about backsliding. I've found one of the truest signs that you are backsliding and that you should probably take another look at where you're headed is how you feel. Unlike with detours that momentarily feel right, when you are backsliding you will feel very unsettled.

Even though my commitment to "Ministry Fridays" was incredibly short-lived, once I had a taste of what it felt like to say yes to beginning to lead my authentic life, it was impossible for me to go back to the way things were before without feeling deeply dissatisfied. This can be a gauge for you as well. There is so much positive energy when you say yes to what you feel called to do that everything else will feel unacceptable. You've given power to that small voice inside you that knows what you need to be truly happy. You've had a glimpse of the possible. And your small voice that calls you to be authentically you will take on a sense of urgency to help you take the next steps forward. Any time I found myself backsliding, I knew. Even before I was ready to do anything about it, I knew. You will too.

Saying yes involves change and change is not easy. Please accept that backsliding is another inevitable reality when you are building an authentic life. The neural grooves that have been controlling the way you respond to specific triggers don't go away just because you've decided to make this change. Take heart in the fact that typically, when you backslide, you won't be taking two steps forward and three steps back. You are much more likely to take only one step or a half step back before you move forward again.

There are two reasons I've found for backsliding. First, when you backslide, the step you are getting ready to take is probably well outside your comfort zone. It feels scary. And second, you are likely in an early stage of your journey. In either case, feel confident that backsliding is a natural part of the journey. But keep this thought in mind as well. The longer you listen to the voice that encourages you to say yes, the easier it becomes to keep moving forward. It took me awhile to get to the point where I can say that I don't backslide anymore, but now I can tell you it can be done.

Let me close this chapter with this thought. No matter what else is going on in your world today, say this affirmation and own it:

"(your name) is in the house! The One. The Only. The Amazing Me! And the world had better grab a seat. It's about to witness the amazing awakening of an incredible superpower."

# Reflections

*What mind shift would you want to take place on your journey?*

_____

_____

_____

_____


*What trigger would you like to create a new neural groove to overcome?*

_____

_____

_____

_____

_____

*Sally Orcutt*

*Have you already identified any tools that have helped you quiet that negative critiquing voice? (I made a decision to journal.)*

_____

_____

_____

_____

_____

## Chapter 3: Finding Your "is-ness"

Your "is-ness" lies in the place where your values, your passions, and your strengths meet.

*(Sally Orcutt)*

During the months between the time I went back full-time to my corporate job and when I finally left for good, I did a lot of soul searching (along with a lot of suffering from my inability to make a decision). The calling I felt in my dream to leave my corporate job and "help" others was still such a powerful force in my life. I couldn't shake the belief that in my current job, I was not doing what was mine to do at this moment of my life. I asked myself, "What do you really want? What are your absolute goals?" What I found is that my goals were very clear. I wanted to:

- To live at peace with myself, accepting myself.

- To live at peace with others, accepting them as they are.

- To share the gifts I have been given, helping others achieve their dreams.

- To let all that touches my life each day be a part of honoring my "is-ness."

None of these goals required me to leave my current job. There were ways I might have realized these goals in my life as it existed at that time. Except, I couldn't. And the more I learned about who I am, my "is-ness," the clearer it became for me why I needed to make a change.

Let's take a look at the journey to finding your "is-ness."

What do you really want in your life in this moment? What are the three or four goals you would like to achieve at this moment of your life?

_____

_____

_____

_____

_____

My company Stretch 4 Success was born from my desire to be all that God has called me to be. It felt aligned with the four goals I had identified for my life. I decided that I would use my marketing skills to help women achieve their goals. So, when a friend of mine suggested I join Women in Networking (WIN), it seemed like a good idea. Each WIN chapter works in this way: there are a number of business categories, each one represented by only one member. That way, you are not competing for business with other members of your chapter. Initially, I went to a meeting at a chapter close to where I live, but there was already someone in the marketing seat.

That led me to Cary, North Carolina, which was about 40 minutes away from my home. They were a fairly new chapter and had an opening in that seat. After eight months in WIN, during which time I helped a number of people as a marketing coach, I felt the now familiar small voice tell me "There's more for you to do." I've learned, as I did when I made the decision to become a Lay Dominican, saying yes is about giving that small voice, *a voice*. I couldn't put my finger on what was next just yet, but I would soon. God clearly puts people in our path that we need to meet. Joining the Cary chapter of WIN led me to Sterling. She is one of the people who helped usher me along on my own path.

As I mentioned earlier, Sterling is a life coach and the author of *The Brain Trust Planner*. Her work centers around aligning your goals with your core values. I was drawn to the idea of uncovering your core values. For me, knowing who you are at your very core is even bigger than alignment with goals. It's about alignment with your life. Understanding your core values is the first step to understanding your unique gifts, what I refer to as your "is-ness." Sterling and I began working together. I helped her with marketing. She shared her insights on how to identify core values.

Core values are not the values that society tells you that you *should* want or have. They are not the values you believe you *should* desire to live by. They are the values that drive and define who you are at your deepest levels. The unique combination of your core values and your life experiences make you who you are—your "is-ness." Being clear on your core values makes it easy to see when you are living in alignment with who you are.

In this chapter, you are going to uncover your authentic "is-ness." As you walk through these steps, let me impress upon you the importance of taking some time to be quiet. The loud voice that continues to be triggered by those old neural pathways can be silenced. But it takes spending time in silence to give your small voice a chance to be heard. For me, that small voice is God or Spirit. However you think of that small voice, I'm sure you've heard it, even if, like me, you have not always listened to it.

## Discovering your "is-ness"

Sterling introduced me to the following list of core values:

# Core Values

| | | | |
|---|---|---|---|
| Accepting | Commitment | Fun-loving | Passionate |
| Accountability | Community | Genuineness | Peace |
| Adventurous | Compassion | Giving | Positive |
| Appreciation | Competence | Gratitude | Presence |
| Athletic | Complacency | Growth | Purposeful |
| Awe | Composure | Healthy | Relationship |
| Balance | Concentration | Honest | Reliable |
| Beauty | Confidence | Hope | Resilient |
| Benevolence | Conformity | Humor | Respected |
| Blissfulness | Connection | Independent | Respectful |
| Boldness | Consciousness | Industriousness | Service |
| Bravery | Consistency | Innovative | Simplicity |
| Brilliance | Contentment | Inspiring | Spiritual |
| Buoyancy | Courageous | Integrity | Spontaneity |
| Calmness | Creative | Intellect | Structure |
| Camaraderie | Curiosity | Intimacy | Supportive |
| Candor | Dependable | Introspective | Togetherness |
| Capability | Determination | Introversion | Truth |
| Care | Direct | Kindness | Unique |
| Certainty | Educated | Laughter | _____ |
| Challenge | Efficient | Listening | _____ |
| Charity | Empathy | Love | _____ |
| Charm | Encourage- | Loyal | _____ |
| Cheerfulness | ment | Marriage | _____ |
| Clarity | Entrepreneurial | Motivate | _____ |
| Classy | Enterprising | Nonconformity | _____ |
| Cleanliness | Extroversion | Nourishing | _____ |
| Cleverness | Faith | Nurturing | _____ |
| Closeness | Family | Open-minded | _____ |
| Cognizance | Fashion | Optimistic | _____ |
| Comfort | Frugality | Organization | _____ |

There are more than 100 core values listed on this sheet with space to add some of your own if needed. Go ahead and review the full list. Be aware of your feelings and emotions surrounding certain words. Allow yourself to feel the energy associated with each word. Your goal for this exercise is to uncover your Top 10 Core Values.

Don't rush the process. Identifying your core values is not something to be checked off so you can move on. This is the first step in finding your "is-ness." Go ahead and give yourself the time you need. Then, circle or write down the values that mean the most to you right now. Mark any word that has an emotional impact on you. We'll bring this back to your Top 10 later, so don't be surprised if you circle more than ten on your list or try to combine a couple of words that feel really similar to you. Everybody does. Remember, if there is a core value that is missing from this list but is important to you, please add it on one of the lines provided and circle it.

How many words did you circle? How many did you try to combine? Were there any core values you were surprised to see missing from your list? There are no *correct* core values that should appear on your list. However, it is very common to initially circle some core values that you believe *should* be on your list. Let me explain.

The first time I selected my Top 10 list, some of the most prominent values I felt were missing were:

- Family

- Spiritual

- Love

That made me uncomfortable. I love my family. How could my list be complete without having family and love on the list? I'm a Lay Dominican Preacher. How could spiritual not have made the cut? I went back and crossed off some of the ones I had and added those into my list. After all, what would people think if they saw that these values were not on my Top 10 list? See how easy it is for the inner critic to take control?

As I got ready to move on to the next step of uncovering my "is-ness," I looked at my list again. I thought about moments in my life that felt most real and honest to me. Moments when I felt most truly happy and at peace. Moments where I felt compelled to step outside my comfort zone and speak up. What was happening in those moments? How did the events in those moments relate to this list of core values? What I discovered was that the three core values I crossed off the list were more "who I was" than the three I added for the sake of appearances. It is not that family, love, and spirituality are not important to me. They are. But it was a real aha moment for me as I realized that my spirituality and the way I love family are demonstrated through the other core values I selected.

With this idea in mind, look at your list again and see if you can bring your list back to ten core values. As you do this, reflect on how each of these values has shown up in your life up to this time. Equally important, think about times when you felt that something in your life was out of alignment or unsettled. One way to discover your core values is to recognize strong emotions when one of these values seems to be under attack.

Let me share with you two stories to illustrate this point. When I was eight years old, another girl and I were talking during class. It was one of those times when our primary teacher switched with another second grade teacher for a particular subject. When my teacher came back to the room, she called me out into the hallway. She told me I was to go and apologize to the other teacher for being disruptive in her class. I don't remember the exact words I used, but basically I said, "Of course, I would do that, but I feel Carolyn should apologize as well." I was about as meek a child as there was, so I feel pretty sure I would not have said this in an aggressive or rude manner. The teacher's reaction shocked me. She hauled me down to the principal's office where I was informed that I was a bold, fresh thing, and they should throw me out of the school. (Yes, I know it sounds a little over the top. I should add that I went to Catholic school in the 1960s.) Since I did not want to get thrown out of school, I went back and apologized to the teacher whose class I had disturbed. I have never forgotten that event. It clearly reveals two of my core values. I was being *honest*. And, it felt wrong and *unfair* to me that I should be punished while Carolyn was not.

The other story I'll share with you happened when I was a senior in high school. I was hanging out in the senior lounge, which was nothing more than an open hallway overlooking the cafeteria. A girl I knew, although I didn't know her well, was sitting there going on and on talking negatively about herself. She was telling us that she was overweight, not at all pretty, and wasn't at all surprised that nobody would ask her out on a date. Did I mention that I was incredibly shy? After a little while, I had heard enough, and I had to speak up. I turned to her and said, "Don't put yourself down. There will always be people who will be quick to do that for you. Don't do it to yourself." I remember speaking those words as if I'd just said them, but only now, as an adult, can appreciate where they came from. I hate to see people hurting; my *nurturer* and *encourager* wanted to help that girl to feel more positive about herself.

There always will be times in our lives when our core values are challenged. There will be times you slip into allowing your negative voice to take control. What I've found is that understanding your core values and *seeing* and *feeling* the moments you have lived those values have tremendous power. *I know who I am.* This has helped me understand clearly why I feel out of alignment sometimes with the events in my life. I am much quicker now to realize when I am being non-authentic. Knowing who I am makes it easier to pull away from the times when my inner critic tries to convince me not to share the gifts I know are mine to share.

# Reflections

*Can you think of some moments in your life where your core values showed up? Take a moment and write down at least one event that supports your core values.*

_____

_____

_____

_____

_____

*Take a moment and write down at least one life event that was difficult for you because it didn't support your core values?*

_____

_____

_____

_____

_____

_____

# Chapter 4: What's Your Superpower?

You're going to make a difference. A lot of times it won't be huge, it won't be visible even. But it will matter just the same.

*(Commissioner Gordon, "Batman")*

**N**ow that you have identified your Top 10 core values, are you ready to identify your superpower?

Your superpower is linked to your core values and life experiences. Let's start by going back to your Top 10 core values. What were the images that came to mind for you as you circled each of your words? Was there a time that quickly came to mind in which that core value was involved? Remember my story about talking in second grade? My core values of honesty and fairness felt as though they were under attack. In fact, as I thought back on my life, I started remembering other times when I felt the same way. This was another aha moment for me. While it would probably bother me if someone was not loyal, I felt outrage at someone being unfair. It's all about core values.

Let's look quickly at Christy's story before we explore our superpowers. It's a wonderful story. One of Christy's core values is *service*. During college she was incredibly involved in campus ministry. She shared with me that after college she felt frustrated because she really wanted to do something to serve God in a big way and nothing she tried seemed to fit. That feeling certainly sounded familiar to me. She knew there was so much need in the world, and she wanted to do something to help. She had always wanted to travel. So, she sought out a position as a missionary in Africa. She worked hard to line up all the funding and grants she needed to fund her trip. She was excited at the thought of all the good work she could do there.

Then, without notice, the whole trip fell apart. She was unable to go. She had been so convinced that she was *supposed* to go to Africa that she found herself falling into a deep depression. Several months later she received an opportunity to go to Australia and serve as an au pair. "No. That can't be where I am being called to serve," she shared. She felt she needed to be helping the poor. But the idea took hold of her and wouldn't let go. Australia? Mmmm. What if? What Christy came to realize and what I want to share with you is that whatever you are doing using your "is-ness" is God's work for you in this moment.

Everything fell into place for her trip to Australia. She felt peaceful and content. She found a way to serve others and travel at the same time. In my experience, when you feel that strong sense of peace, it is the surest way to know that you are on the right path.

Christy's path took her on a pretty big trip. For most of us, finding the opportunity to share our "is-ness" will be found right in our own communities. Perhaps even within our own families.

To help visualize your superpower, let's identify specific instances where you have *shown up* in your life in response to your core values. In the first column of Table 4.2 (following), go ahead and put each of the ten core values you identified earlier. In the next column, please write one situation in which you feel that this core value was visible to others. The time frame is unimportant. These moments can be from yesterday or ten years ago. The important part is to be as specific as you can about what you were doing in that moment. In the last column, go ahead and list the name of the person who was impacted by the moment you described. If you cannot remember the individual's name, that's fine. Just do the best you can. For example, the sister of my friend Sue or the guy my friend Tom brought to the meeting or, maybe, a woman I met in the parking lot. I've given you an example to get started.

## Table 4.1: Sample Core Value Entry

| Core Value | Your action linked to your core value | Who was impacted? |
|---|---|---|
| Nurturing | Senior year in high school when I heard a classmate putting themselves down. I reminded them that there will always be people willing to do that to them. They should not do it to themselves. | Liz P. |

## Table 4.2: Core Value Sheet

| Core Value | Your action linked to your core value | Who was impacted? |
|---|---|---|
| | | |
| | | |
| | | |
| | | |
| | | |
| | | |
| | | |
| | | |
| | | |
| | | |

Were any of the people on your list random individuals such as someone you met in the grocery store? Maybe a woman whose crying child needed distracting while she tried to check out her books in the library? Was there someone at your job?

When you live authentically, you positively touch the lives of others everywhere you go. You may never know the impact of sharing your "is-ness" with the people you meet. I hope that my words were encouraging to Liz. I hope she felt uplifted because somebody who didn't even know her very well took the time to validate her. I know that, as shy as I was, I felt compelled to speak to her. Letting your "is-ness" touch the lives of others can be like that. You won't always know the impact of your words or actions, but you will feel energized when you are authentic.

**What sharing your "is-ness" looks like**

Let's look at several other stories of women who were "just sharing their gifts" and were surprised to see they were having an impact. What do they have in common? Each of them try to be present as they go through their day. Are they able to do this all the time? No. But when they do, it gives them the chance to share their gifts in the most unexpected places. Like them, you will see opportunities to share your gifts just by getting out of your own head and really seeing what is going on around you. You probably already do this sometimes. You just may not have thought about it that way.

I met Tonya when I joined Women in Networking (WIN) after starting my own business. She has been such a gift in my life. I was struggling to communicate with the members of the group about how I could help them in their businesses. Coming from the corporate world, I overcomplicated my message. Tonya reached out, and we had a terrific conversation just to get to know each other.

We learned more about each other in the 45 minutes we spoke than I would have imagined. And then we started talking about our businesses. Tonya is an insurance agent. During our conversation she shared with me that she loves to help people. At least twice a month, she said, people who come in to speak to her about insurance end up telling her everything about themselves including some very painful experiences. She told me they often share so much that at the end of the conversation they say to her, "I don't know why I told you all of that." I do. Tonya's core values include *listening*, *caring*, and *genuineness*. People can tell she has a caring heart. You feel safe sharing your life story with her. By the way, she also helped me get my message right!

Remember Karen? She has a real gift for helping people to verbalize difficult emotions. She uses this gift in her family, with friends, as a Spiritual Director, and as an Al Anon sponsor. In fact, she has been sharing this gift with others since she was a teenager. Still, she didn't feel as though she was sharing anything. She told me she used to feel very frustrated because she longed to find her "big why" or purpose. She used words like, "I'm just…" and "All I do is…"

Thankfully, she had the chance to speak with someone whose gifts must have included *wisdom*. He told her that her gifts seemed inconsequential to her because they came naturally. Understanding this has helped Karen feel liberated from the voice in her head that told her to measure herself against what she "might have done" and know that just being Karen is all she ever needs to be. Her superpower is *presence*.

Nancy really enjoys bringing people together. She shared with me that one of the most satisfying experiences she recalls was in giving someone an opportunity to join her organization. She knew this person was the right candidate even though others weren't so sure. The more we spoke, it was clear that her superpower is *integrity*. Nancy shared with me that even as a child, she pointed out situations where she felt others had not been treated fairly. It was more than honesty for Nancy. It was about "doing the right thing." There have been several instances in her life when those around her told her not to get involved. For Nancy, not getting involved in those circumstances was not an option. Living a life of integrity drives her to do what she believes is the right thing regardless of the consequences.

What about you? Have you ever felt the way these women did? Now that you know your core values, is it possible you have been taking them for granted?

_____

_____

_____

_____

_____

Susan spent her entire childhood feeling invisible. As the youngest of four in a family filled with dysfunction, growing up she often asked herself, "Why doesn't anybody see me for who I am?" She longed to feel as though she mattered. As an adolescent, she made some choices that brought her negative attention. She knew she was not valuing herself as she should, but at least she no longer felt invisible. As an adult, she has found her own value. And her superpower - *thoughtfulness*.

When I asked her if she could recall moments when she felt she had used that superpower, she told me about a woman at the post office. Susan was in line listening to the conversation as an older woman in front of her was trying to mail a pie to her family for the holidays because she couldn't be with them this year. The pie needed to be mailed carefully which led to the cost being much more than the older woman thought it would be and more money than she had with her. Susan didn't get annoyed as she watched the woman dig deep in her purse trying to find enough money to cover the cost. She took a step forward and said to the woman behind the counter, "Let me take care of this." Susan felt the warmth of the woman's smile. They both felt very visible to each other in that moment.

Do you remember a time your core values "showed in public," like Susan's thoughtful action?

_____

_____

_____

_____

_____

## Identifying your superpower?

I began this chapter by telling you that your superpower is linked to your core values. It is all about how you show up for relationships, for work, for God, for life. Now that you've seen at least ten ways in which you have touched the lives of others, and heard some stories of big and small ways others have shared their superpower, let's explore what your superhero looks like. Start by drawing a picture of yourself in the center of the "I am a Superhero" box on the following page. Or, if you prefer, use pictures from magazines to illustrate or write words to describe ways you are living your core values. Get a larger sheet of paper if you wish. Use some of the situations you described in Table 4.2. Add others as they come to you. Are there things in life you would still like to do? Is there something you've dreamed of that you put on hold? Take your time. Let the picture come alive.

What does your superhero look like? What are the ways you have used your core values to make a difference in the world?

# I am a Superhero!

Look at your superhero. What do you see? What was it inside you that had you draw the image you created? What were you feeling? As you look at all the images you've drawn, they will begin to speak to your "big why," your purpose. What is one core value that stands out from the others? Is there one core value that is part of each of the images you've drawn? Our Superhero uses each of our core values, but there is always one that stands out from the rest. That is your *Superpower*.

Here's my Superhero. I've found that my superpower is **kindness**.

Okay, clearly I am not an artist. This picture illustrates my core values of encouragement, accepting, nurturing, dependability, etc. Each image also includes part of what it means to me to be kind. Do you remember what I uncovered about myself after my year-long journey into social justice? I believe each and every one of us is *beloved*. And we are beloved just because *we are*. Treating other people as if they have value and are worthy of my attention and consideration is my definition of being kind.

Being authentic is not a competition. Lots of people are profoundly kind. When I say my superpower is kindness, I am saying that I am my most authentic self when I feel I am being kind to others. And my definition of kindness requires me to be aware of others. It is about looking another person in the eyes, paying attention to the words they say, and listening for the nuances of emotion surrounding their words. Whether it is my family, friends, co-workers, people in the store, the homeless, individuals in prison—I believe they and all individuals are beloved. Not perfect. Sometimes annoying. And always worthy of kindness.

Do you see how I added the "Kindness" flag to my Superhero? Add a flag to your superhero naming your superpower. Take some time and write down how you feel your superpower shows up in each of the images you've drawn.

_____

_____

_____

_____

_____

How will your life be different now that you recognize your superpower? How do you know when you are using it? Will stress and challenges disappear? I'm afraid not. Who you are is who you are. Beloved and imperfect. This means that when you let your superhero shine, you will still make mistakes. You will still do things you wish you hadn't done and say things you wish you hadn't said. That's okay. Part of the power of authenticity is using your superpower and still accepting your imperfections. Focusing on using your superpowers *will* change the way you feel about your imperfect self every day. It will also bring focus to the gift you are for other people in the world.

What are some simple ways you can envision using your superpower each day?

_____

_____

_____

_____

I've found there are plenty of opportunities each day to use my superpower. All I need to do is recognize they are happening and be willing to say yes. That sounds pretty simple, right? It's not always easy. There are still times I am wrapped up in my own head, and I miss the chance to say yes, and there are still times that I hesitate. However, I grow stronger in sharing my "is-ness" each time I say do say yes. And, the funny thing is, the more often I say yes, the more opportunities I see in my life to share that part of my authentic self with others. I've created a simple reminder for myself that I look at every day. It's a magnet that says:

**This colorful magnet (actual size 5.47" x 4.21") has the same colors as the book cover.**

Regardless of how large or small the actions are that we take when we are being authentic, we create energy for ourselves and those around us. Visit my website at *www.stretch4success.com* to get your own "Say Yes" magnet or bookmark.

# Reflections

*How does it feel to claim your superpower? Take a moment and celebrate this wonderful gift only you can share.*

_____

_____

_____

_____

_____

_____

# Chapter 5:
# Why Saying Yes Matters

To each individual, the manifestation

of the Spirit is given for some benefit.

*(1 Cor. 12:7)*

*A*re you starting to feel the energy linked to saying yes to your life? You've identified your core values, pictured your superhero, and identified the ways you are already using your superpowers to make a difference in the lives of others. You may even be seeing opportunities to say yes each day. I'm excited for you. There's more. Choosing to live an authentic life is bigger than you. Why?

*Because you will change the world.*

We all possess and present energy to the world around us every day. What I've found is that energy is filtered through the lens of how we feel about ourselves and our lives. When we love ourselves, when we celebrate who we are and what we have to offer, there is a positive energy that bursts through our eyes, our smile, and our whole being. This energy is contagious. It uplifts the people around you. To truly love yourself, look in the mirror and smile because you know your "is-ness" is unique and is a gift to yourself and others. You need to know, deep within you, that you are loved and lovable. Just the way you are.

What is one area of your life that will be impacted by you saying yes to your life? How will your yes change your relationships with those around you?

*Sally Orcutt*

_____

_____

_____

_____

_____

Once you accept that you have been given the gifts you need to live the life you are called to live and that you are beloved just the way you are, you are ready to see how your gifts fit into the universal whole. For years I compared myself to others. And for years, I felt as though the gifts I had weren't really worth much. Like Karen, I was constantly judging others to try and find a way to feel better about myself. That meant I tried to find their weakness. Not only is this thinking problematic for relationships but because the very act of judging comes from a belief that you are not good enough, you are constantly reminding yourself of that negative belief. That kind of thinking doesn't work. Instead of comparing and judging, St. Paul's letter to the Corinthians suggests,

> *"There are different kinds of gifts but the same Spirit distributes them. There are different kinds of service, but the same Lord...Now to each one the manifestation of the Spirit is given for the common good."*
> *(1 Corinthians 12:4-5, 7)*

This reading goes on to point out the obvious need we have for each other. In verse 15 he writes, 'Now if the foot should say, "Because I am not a hand, I do not belong to the body" it would not for that reason stop being part of the body.' And in verse 21 he writes, 'The eye cannot say to the hand, "I don't need you"! And the head cannot say to the feet, "I don't need you"!' Of course not. In the same way, we are all different from each other. We each have a unique combination of core values and life experiences. It is our "is-ness." And, rather than compare ourselves to others or judge ourselves or them, being authentic lets us own our unique manifestation of the Spirit and use it not only for our own good but also for the common good.

This message is so obvious it is a wonder how difficult it is to see. Our uncertainty about the value of our gifts and our unwillingness to own our voice cheats the world around us of all we have to offer.

When I first started visiting Lyle, a young man on death row at Central Prison in Raleigh, I was uncomfortable but not for the reason that might seem most obvious. I wasn't sure if I knew how to connect with Lyle given the differences in our ages and life experiences. I was extremely nervous, and although I wrote to him regularly, I had avoided actually going to see him. He continued to ask me when I would be able to come. Finally, I put aside my list of excuses and shared why I had not come to see him yet. I shared that I found writing so much easier because it gave me a chance to think about what I would say. It gave me the opportunity to try and find interesting things to talk about with him. I told him that I am really awkward at thinking on my feet, and I was concerned that I would have nothing to say.

He was so incredibly generous. He told me that my caring so much about him and his feelings really touched him. He said that when I shared my struggles with him, I had given him a gift of kindness. And then he said, "Stop worrying. I can hold up my end of a conversation. Please come visit me!" And I did. Through his words, Lyle encouraged me with his gifts of *humor* and *kindness*. I will always remember those words and how they made me feel. Trust that the people with whom you share your gifts will do the same for you.

Our inner critic can be so powerful that we become convinced that who we are and what we have to offer will not be enough. However, when we are consciously living out of our core values, we are more aware. We are able to feel the pleasure of positively impacting another person. The gift of connection stays with us, enriching our lives long after the encounter has passed. Those moments provide us with affirmation that whether we are an arm or a foot, what we have to offer is needed.

Perhaps you are still at the level of believing the fact that you are a gift with your head alone. I ask you to please stick with me. That was my first step as well. It definitely took some time for me to believe in my heart that I am a gift.

Keep your focus on saying yes. Keep asking yourself "what does *yes* look like today"? Once the process of believing begins to take hold, you will be amazed how quickly it picks up speed. These words are true. You are a gift. You are beautifully and wonderfully made. And the gifts you possess are vital to the community in which you live.

Share a time that you felt as though you were a gift to another person. How did that feel?

_____

_____

_____

_____

## What color crayon are you?

What do crayons have to do with the importance of sharing your unique gifts with the people around you? A member of my Lay

Dominican community shared this story with me. "Imagine," he said, "that your very being could be described using a single color. Each of us has a unique color that represents our "is-ness." Every time you share your unique gifts with someone, your color is painted on the canvas of their life. And, when they share their gifts with you, their color is richly added to your life's canvas as well." Imagine your life's canvas looks like a colorful garden, a vibrant rainbow, an exhilarating sunset, whatever image contains a variety of beautiful colors. Now, imagine that each color was added by one individual sharing their unique "is-ness" with you. How would your canvas be different if they hadn't shared those gifts? Think about what an impact your own color makes on the canvases of other people's lives as well.

_____

_____

_____

_____

_____

It is only in sharing our unique gifts or "is-ness" with each other, whether our color is magenta, green, lavender (whatever!), that each of our canvases is filled with all the beautiful and rich colors of nature. Look at the community of people around you—your family, friends, neighbors, co-workers, the people you see at the mall, or at the park. You touch the world around you, person by person. And you are the *only person* who can bring your gifts the way you bring them. Even if there are 100, 1,000, or 10,000 people who have the same Top 10 core values as you. Each of us has our own superpower because our core values are influenced by our life experience. And no two people, even siblings from the same family, have the same life experience. That makes each person's "is-ness" unique.

It is so easy to miss how important we are to others. I love this quote by Fred Rogers (Mister Rogers' Neighborhood), *"If only you could sense how important you are to the lives of those you meet; how important you can be to people you may never even dream of. There is something of yourself that you leave at every meeting with another person."*

When I was desperately trying to stay at my last job even when I knew I needed to leave and do something else, I was definitely leaving something of myself with those around me. Negative energy. I didn't see the people around me. I was blind to even the most obvious opportunities to share a kind word with others. I didn't see them. I was spending all my time looking inward. And, no matter how hard I tried, I couldn't let go of the feeling I wasn't being true to myself. It left me feeling frustrated and unhappy. I wasn't being kind to myself or anyone else. I wasn't being deliberately mean. I simply wasn't bringing my "is-ness." My color was nowhere to be found.

How do you bring your color to the canvas of the people around you? Are you the one that brings life to the party because you are spontaneous? Do you help your church or your child's school because you have so many innovative ideas? Are you, like Tonya, the person others seek out when they need to talk because you are a good listener? Or, are you the one that people call because they "always feel better" after they talk to you?

_____

_____

_____

_____

_____

However you bring your color, keep doing it and know you are making a difference. Here's another visual for you: have you ever tried to print something when your printer was running low on one of the color cartridges? What happens? The picture comes out looking bland and lifeless. That is what happens to the people around you when your color is not added to their canvas. Say yes and bring your color every day.

**A time to reflect**

Now I'd like you to take some time to reflect more deeply on the notes you just jotted down. I can tell you how important it is to bring your unique color to the canvases of the people around you, but I'm convinced we integrate ideas into our thinking when we can see them clearly in our own lives. Think about the people you came into contact with this past week. Start close to home with family and then broaden out to friends, co-workers, acquaintances, and then people you just happen to see in the places you visit. Describe the moments you drew on another person's canvas. In what ways did you share your "is-ness?"

_____

_____

_____

Next, I want you to think about each of those individuals. Believe that, as Mr. Rogers says, you've left something of yourself with them. What would have been different for *them* if you had not entered into their lives and brought your "is-ness"? What would have been missing for them if you felt you had nothing to add and kept silent? At one of my speaking engagements recently, I asked people in the audience to share one of their gifts. I heard things like sharing their music, being an encourager, a teacher. Next, I asked them to think about one person whose life would have been different if they had not shared their gifts with that person. Slowly, a look of understanding came across their faces. They knew they had touched lives and made a difference. Take a moment and reflect on how the lives of the people you identified above would have been different if you had not shared your gifts with them.

Remember, your "is-ness" matters. You have unique gifts and the world needs you to share them.

**Are you ready?**

Are you ready to take the next steps and see where your unique gifts can take you? Are you ready to let your Superhero picture come alive? Let's continue the journey together!

## Chapter 6:
## Unleashing Your Superhero

We don't meet people by accident.
They are meant to cross our paths
for a reason.

*(Lessons Learned in Life)*

*I*s your superhero ready to start flexing its muscles? Grab your cape. Grab your superhero boots. This chapter offers you some practical tips for the next steps on the journey. They are the steps I continue to follow as I look for my next yes each day.

## Keep listening to your authentic voice

*A*s you grow in living your authentic life, find a way to create and maintain balance. Once you find your authentic voice, commit to finding time to continue listening to it. I get busy sometimes and lose sight of taking the quiet time I need. It happens. If you find yourself feeling overwhelmed or unsettled, just stop, listen, and make some adjustments.

When I first discovered that my superpower was kindness, I drew the many different ways I felt that I could use that gift to live an authentic life. Many of the images in the picture I drew were things I was doing already in some way even if I was not consistent in doing them. Although I wanted to unleash my superpower, it was important to me that I did not lose sight of the ways I was already being authentic. As I began to work on helping women entrepreneurs achieve their goals using my skills and knowledge as a marketing professional, I was so excited about this next step in my journey that I often allowed myself to become overly scheduled. I scheduled appointments back to back to back, often not allowing more than the minimum amount of time to get from one place to the next. I thought I was doing the right thing. People were asking for my help. The more appointments I could schedule, the more people I could help. Right? Not exactly. I became increasing stressed because I had stretched myself too thin. Although I continued to help my small business clients, the stress I caused myself by overcommitting impacted many of my relationships. I soon realized this behavior was not sustainable.

Things got even more hectic as I began to explore my desire to use my superpowers to offer workshops about finding your authentic voice and living the life you are called to live. I still wanted to help small businesses as a marketing coach and, quite honestly, needed to do so financially. In my head, I believed I could do it all. Of course, I was overscheduled with client appointments, *and* I was trying to find time to build a workshop presentation and market that presentation. I was excited and energized by the work I was doing but, as you can imagine, this only decreased any sense of balance I had in my life.

Not only did this overscheduling and work on my presentation result in greater stress for me each day but I stopped doing some of the very things that I enjoyed doing that made me feel authentic. Over a six-month period, I stopped serving meals to the homeless and in women's shelters and almost completely curtailed my visits to my friend Lyle in prison. These were activities that had been on my list of how I was already living my authentic life. How could I give them up? I thought about doing these things. And I told myself that I would get started again soon. But each month there was always something else that I felt needed to be done, and I didn't listen to my authentic voice.

If finding our authentic voice requires us to have some practice of silence, continual listening to our authentic voice forces us to make that time as well. The more excited I got about the work I was trying to do, the more sporadic became my practice of finding time to be quiet. Instead of letting myself be led by my authentic voice, I just started charging down the path I had identified. My authentic voice may have led me to the path, but then I turned off the connection and kept going. That is why I encourage you to continue to find time to be intentional about listening. What usually hits my reset button is feeling overwhelmed; it forces me to take a step back and breathe. I get quiet again and give my authentic voice a chance to be heard. It is always very fruitful for me. In the silence I look at where I am and then re-evaluate and re-prioritize what I am doing.

**Inventory your skills**

You've imagined some actions or steps you want to take to unleash your superhero. They call to you and you sense this is the direction you want your life to take. Where you are today? Like the skills I possessed in marketing, what skills do you have that will be useful to you along this journey?

_____

_____

_____

_____

_____

In my work as a marketing coach, I felt I possessed most of the skills I needed to do that work. Naturally, it was important to continue to attend workshops and read material to stay current and continue to learn. But for the specific work I was doing for my clients, I had a lot of expertise. However, the more I felt called to do workshop presentations on authenticity, the more I realized that I had some skills I needed to grow. I was passionate about my topic and confident that it was a story that I not only wanted to share but that I felt would benefit many people. Public speaking, however, would be something new for me.

I decided to join Toastmasters to get more comfortable with public speaking. I looked around for a club whose members were public speakers. It made sense to me to surround myself with individuals who spoke for a living. I was drawn to one that seemed like the right people, and it met at a time that was convenient for me. I went to visit. The first time I went, I felt as though I were back in high school. I was overwhelmed and definitely out of my comfort zone. The day I showed up, I saw that one of the members was a speaker one of my clients had hired to speak at their annual event. All I could think was, "What am I doing here?" This is where having my vision for the next steps of my authentic journey really helped me.

I was sure preparing my workshop presentation was the next step on my journey. So uncomfortable or not, I needed to be there. I joined the club and after being an observer for the first month or so, I jumped in to give my first speech to this audience of professional speakers. I did a short piece from my proposed workshop presentation on authenticity. I got some excellent feedback as well as some incredibly positive comments. They saw me as one of them. I am one of them. And in that moment, all of the nervousness I had in taking this next step to help me accomplish what I truly believed was part of my journey was gone, and in its place was the confidence that I could do this, and I was on the right path.

Then I started talking to Kevin, one of the members of the club, about the value to my work of writing a book. A book. I have often thought about writing a book but had never been dedicated or disciplined enough to do so. Kevin shared with me the value to his speaking career of having a book and suggested I consider writing one. Being a writer was not a skill I even considered I would need as I continued on my journey toward being a workshop leader. But his arguments made a lot of sense. I signed up for a class on writing a book that I believed would offer me tips, advice, and structure. It did all of that, and more. This book is the result of that class and the next one is already floating around in my head. There are other skills I am learning I need that I had not even considered. None of them are things I cannot do. They are just skills I have not mastered yet. But I can, as long as I stay open to where I am being led.

What skills do you want to nurture and develop further?

_____

_____

_____

_____

_____

## Watch out, the floodgates are about to open

If you stay open, people and opportunities will enter your life that will be incredible. So, be ready. And remember, with everyone who comes into your life to walk with you on this path, listen to your authentic voice to try and discern if the fork in the road you are taking is the direction you want to go. Also remember, it is natural to start down some paths that are not for you. They may seem right at the time partly because the people involved are people you admire and the work seems aligned with what you are trying to do. As we discussed before, trust your instincts. Keep listening to your authentic voice and stay focused on where your superhero is headed. That voice will serve to bring you back should you head down a path that is not really for you.

Remember what I told you about my work with Sterling. As much as I enjoyed the work we were doing together, my small voice kept telling me this was not the next step for me. As difficult as it was for me at that time to say no to Sterling, my authentic voice reminded me that I needed to speak and share my message on the power of leading an authentic life. While the work Sterling was doing was aligned with that message, it was not the same message. The ability to make that decision was yet another confirmation of the power of living my authentic life. The old Sally, the woman who believed she needed to bend herself into a pretzel to please others and be worthy, was slipping further and further away. Knowing who I am and the gifts I am being called to share gave me the power to walk away.

Has there been a time when you have linked yourself to someone else's dream instead of your own?

_____

_____

_____

_____

_____

What caused you to realize you had headed down the wrong path for you?

_____

_____

_____

_____

_____

**Find an accountability partner**

Stephanie is a good friend and also my accountability partner. As accountability partners, we continue to support and push each other to keep moving forward on the work we are trying to do. Have you ever worked with an accountability partner? If not, I encourage you to find one. Although Stephanie and I share a common desire to speak and write, you and your accountability partner do not need to be that aligned. The most important aspect of the relationship is that you can be honest with each other. We all make excuses when we are unsure about what to do next or when we are stepping outside our comfort zone. Your accountability partner will hold your feet to the fire and challenge you to ask yourself why you are not moving forward.

Your accountability partner can help add balance as you work to accomplish your dreams. I took the StrengthsFinder test several years ago. Unlike your "is-ness," your strengths are linked to your skills and talents. Are you someone whose strengths include building relationships, thinking up new ideas, seeing the connections between ideas, or getting things done? What I found is that one of my top strengths is *achiever*. I find it easy to stay focused working toward my goals. Stephanie is an "idea" person. We kid about the fact that her mind is constantly popping out new ideas. The balance between the two of us is yet another way we help each other. She helps me stretch my thinking; I help her stay on track toward accomplishing her goals. As you unleash your superhero, work with your accountability partner to help you keep reaching for your dreams. I encourage you to take the Strengthsfinder test along with your accountability partner. Doing so will help you put together a strategy for taking advantage of your individual strengths.

How do you think an accountability partner could help you in your next steps?

_____

_____

_____

_____

_____

## Enjoy the journey

*— Life is a journey and not a destination. —*

*A*s you continue to unleash the power of the superhero within you, know that you will still have days that you will fall back into old habits and thought patterns. The difference is now you know how to say no to them. You have seen all the ways in which you are already leading an authentic life using the gifts you have to make a difference for yourself and those around you. You have seen the faces of the people whose lives you have impacted by using your gifts. They have names. And you realize the difference it would have made in their lives if you had not shared your gifts with them.

Once you know something, you can never un-know it. This means that even on your worst day, there will still be a glimmer of light that will call you back to your true self.

Enjoy the journey. I'm not sure there is an ultimate or final destination. Although I enjoy the peace of living my authentic life each day, new possibilities continue to present themselves to me. They lead me further and further along a path that continues to offer me opportunities to share my "is-ness" in the world. It's fun and exciting.

I look back sometimes on my life before I understood how important it is for me to live authentically and share my authentic self with the people I meet. I smile as I remember the people whose lives I did touch in ways that changed both of our lives. It gives me joy and contentment to know that even before I realized what my superpower was, I was using it to make a difference. You have used yours too. The life of your dreams is entirely within your grasp. Say yes 2 your life and love the "is-ness" that is your gift to the world.

I'll close this chapter with this thought. As you embark on this journey to authenticity, I think the most exciting realization of all is understanding that living the life of your dreams is entirely up to you. You have everything you need within in you, and the world needs you to share your wonderful gifts.

# *Epilogue*

Your talent is God's gift to you; what you do with it is your gift to God.

*(Leo Buscaglia)*

Ten years ago as I began this journey, I asked a good friend how I could be sure that I was following my true path. It's funny, today, I would offer the same answer she gave me that day. "There is no path really. We make the path taking one step at a time. However, when things fall into place and you meet people that connect with you and encourage you, when the world seems to be co-creating with you at every turn, you can be pretty sure you are where you are supposed to be." Based on my experience, this is true.

This journey to living my authentic life has been wonderful. Each day I wake up knowing why I am here. I love the work I am doing and seek only to find new ways to share this message and new individuals to uplift or encourage. I have a great deal of energy and passion, and sometimes I overwhelm myself because my heart wants to do more than my mind and body can manage. That's when I take a step back, look at what I'm doing, get quiet, and ask God to help me see if I'm taking the reins too much trying to do this work. I want to do the work He is calling me to do. And that work will never be too much.

That night in my dream, it was clear to me that God was reaching out and saying, "Please stop. We both know this life is not working. I've got something so much better for you. And you're the only one who can do it the way I need it to be done." I have come to realize that to do the work I believe God is calling me to do, I just need to get out of the way and let Him do His thing. This thinking helps me every time my comfort zone needs expanding. Even though in the moment I sometimes think, "Really? I need to do what?" Then I keep going. And I'm never disappointed. There is always a strength I gain from these moments.

Understanding who I am and celebrating my "is-ness" continues to be a gift for me. When I started looking at my core values and seeing how I had been sharing my "is-ness" even during the years that I was so filled with doubt, it was very emotional for me. I saw that the path I'd taken was the path I needed to walk. My own lived moments of self-doubt have led to my deep resolve to help others move past their self-doubt moments.

My new life began the day my mom died. And while I am forever thankful for the gift of the love and friendship we shared, I am also deeply grateful for the life I now have. During her life, my mom showed me all that I was and her words are what I now claim. She was my champion and whenever I would try to play it safe, she would be right beside me telling me that I could do anything I wanted to do. I will never forget the words she said to me during the last years of her life. Do you remember the movie *Beaches* from 1989 with Bette Midler and Barbara Hershey? It's the story of two very dear friends. Just like mom and me. The soundtrack includes:

> *"You were content to let me shine. That's your way. You always walked a step behind. Did you ever know that you're my hero? You're everything I would like to be. I could fly higher than an eagle, you are the wind beneath my wings."*

Out of nowhere one afternoon my mom said to me, "You are the wind beneath my wings." My mom was the most amazing woman I have ever known. She was also a woman who struggled with addiction for many years and felt deeply undeserving of love and applause. She saw the pain she knew her behavior caused. But too often that is all she saw. I saw and felt the pain too, but I always saw so much more. She was my hero. I wanted her to know that she was absolutely beautiful and wonderful no matter what. When she said those words to me, I knew she felt the unconditional acceptance and love I gave her. My eyes still tear up when I think of that moment, but it also makes me smile. I have dedicated this book to my mom. She gave me so much. She helped me see who I was before I was ready to own it and see it for myself. Today, I own all that I am. And I seek to be "the wind beneath the wings" of others wherever I can.

Thank you for taking this journey with me. Please connect with me on Facebook at **www.facebook.com/stretch4success/**. I'd like to hear all that your Superhero is up to!

# Resources

*The Power of Habit* by Charles Duhigg

Just Faith Program — **http://justfaith.org/programs/**

Lay Dominican Life — **http://domlife.org/dominican-family/laity/**

*The Brain Trust Planner* by Sterling M. Fulton, MHA

Core Value Identification Worksheet — additional copies available at **www.stretch4success.com**

StrengthsFinder — **http://www.strengthstest.com/**

*Say Yes 2 Your Life: Your Journey* by Mrs. Sally Orcutt, OP — a journal companion to *Say Yes 2 Your life: Journey to Celebrate Your "is-ness,"* available on **Amazon.com**

## About the Author

Mrs. Sally Orcutt, OP

Sally Orcutt is a speaker, author, and workshop leader. As a lay member of the Order of Preachers, or Dominicans, Sally is a voice of encouragement for those trying to breakthrough self-imposed barriers to celebrate the gifts they have been given. In this, her first book, she offers readers a roadmap for their own journey to stop making comparisons and celebrate their "is-ness." Sally enjoys offering workshops and presentations to empower audiences to discover their unique gifts. Her Signature Presentation is titled: "Unleash the Superhero Within You." As a companion to this book, Sally has published a journal that offers additional questions to consider as you journey to Say Yes 2 Your Life. The journal titled, *Say Yes 2 Your Life: Your Journey* is available on Amazon.

Sally and her husband Paul live in Raleigh, North Carolina, with their wonderful, if crazy, dog Stevie. They enjoy visiting her two grown sons in Charlotte, North Carolina, and New York City as often as possible. For more information, visit her website at **stretch4success.com**